W9-AWC-879

For Pam and her grandchildren, Amelia, Dashel, and Leo.
May your growing pod leap, swim, and play together like dolphins.

—C.R. and P.R.

Photo credits
Cover/title page: © Debra McGuire/iStockphoto.com
Pages 4–11: © Augusto Stanzani/Ardea; 12–13: © Charlie Phillips/age fotostock;
14–15: © Kevin Schafer/Alamy; 16–17: © František Czanner/iStockphoto.com;
18–19: © Auscape/Ardea; 20: © George Clerk/iStockphoto.com; 21: © Steve Bloom Images/Alamy;
22: © Valerie Taylor/Ardea; 23–25: © François Gohier/Ardea; 26–27: © Augusto Stanzani/Ardea;
28–29: © Blair Howard/iStockphoto.com; 30–31 © Tom and Pat Leeson/Ardea;
32: Photo by Molly Leff © American Museum of Natural History.

Scholastic is constantly working to lessen the environmental impact of our manufacturing processes.
To view our industry-leading paper procurement policy, visit www.scholastic.com/paperpolicy.

Designed by Amy Wahlfield.

No part of this publication may be reproduced in whole or in part, or stored in a retrieval system,
or transmitted in any form or by any means, electronic, mechanical, photocopying, recording,
or otherwise, without written permission of the publisher. For information regarding permission,
write to Sterling Publishing Company, Inc., 387 Park Avenue South, New York, NY 10016.

Text copyright © 2011 by Sterling Publishing Company, Inc. and the American Museum of Natural History.
All rights reserved. Published by Scholastic Inc., 557 Broadway, New York, NY 10012,
by arrangement with Sterling Publishing Company, Inc.
Printed in the U.S.A.

ISBN-13: 978-0-545-49671-1
ISBN-10: 0-545-49671-3

SCHOLASTIC and associated logos are trademarks
and/or registered trademarks of Scholastic Inc.

18 19 20   40   21 20

AMERICAN MUSEUM OF NATURAL HISTORY

Baby Dolphin's FIRST DAY

Peter and Connie Roop

SCHOLASTIC INC.
New York Toronto London Auckland
Sydney New Delhi Hong Kong

A baby dolphin is born in the ocean.

His mother takes care of him.

They swim together.

Dolphins must breathe air.

The baby dolphin takes his first breath.

He breathes through a blowhole.

It is on top of his head.

The mother dolphin whistles
to her baby.
The baby learns his mother's call.

He swims close to her.

The baby dolphin will soon learn
to whistle back.

The baby dolphin is hungry.

He drinks milk from his mother.

The mother is hungry, too.

She has found a fish to eat.

Dolphins live in every ocean.

Some dolphins live in rivers, too.

These are Amazon river dolphins.

Dolphins are some of the smartest animals in the water.

Dolphins swim together.

Their group is called a pod.

The pod swims fast.

The dolphins jump into the air.

They land in the water.

SPLASH!

Danger! There is a shark!

The baby swims closer to his mother.

The dolphins swim away.

The baby is safe.

A dolphin swims next to the baby
and his mother.

She helps care for the baby.

She is the baby's "aunt."

The dolphins swim almost all day long.

They leap. They dive. They move.

The baby needs to rest.

Dolphins take many short naps.

Dolphins must be awake to breathe.
They must swim to the top of the ocean
to breathe air.

The sun sets.

Baby dolphin's first day ends.

Tomorrow will be another busy day.

MEET THE EXPERT!

My name is **Neil Duncan**, and I am a biologist. I work for the Division of Vertebrate Zoology at the American Museum of Natural History in New York City. As a collections manager, I get to work with all kinds of animal specimens that have been gathered from around the world.

The natural world has always been a passion of mine, and I have traveled all over the United States to study animals. In California, I researched small forest mammals called fishers and martens; I helped protect endangered shorebirds from human disturbance and from predators in New York; and I have studied many other wildlife species, including fish and whitetail deer.

I received my Bachelor of Science degree in Wildlife and Fisheries Biology from the University of Vermont, and now I am earning my Master's degree from Hofstra University in New York. I am currently studying a species of turtle called the diamondback terrapin. I enjoy learning about diamondback terrapins because they are strong and hardy creatures, and they have managed to survive right near New York City.

If you are interested in biology, one thing you could do is volunteer for a local wildlife organization to learn what kind of animals live in your area. The world of animals is fascinating!